Also by Joseph Donahue

POETRY AND CHAPBOOKS

Before Creation

Monitions of the Approach

World Well Broken

Terra Lucida

Terra Lucida XVI–XX

Incidental Eclipse

In This Paradise

The Copper Scroll

Terra Lucida

Dissolves

Red Flash on a Black Field

ANTHOLOGIES

*Primary Trouble: An Anthology of
   Contemporary American Poetry*

*The World in Time and Space: Towards a History
   of Innovative American Poetry in Our Time*

DARK CHURCH

JOSEPH DONAHUE

DARK CHURCH

TERRA LUCIDA IX–XII

VERGE BOOKS

PUBLISHED BY VERGE BOOKS

WWW.VERGEBOOKS.COM

ISBN 978-0-9889885-2-1

DESIGN AND COMPOSITION BY QUEMADURA

PRINTED ON ACID-FREE, RECYCLED PAPER

IN THE UNITED STATES OF AMERICA

Acknowledgments: the epigraph and a number of the lines quoted in the suite titled "dark church" are taken from *Rosestrikes and Coffee Grinds* by Seyhan Erözçelik, translated by Murat Nemet-Nejat, Talisman House, 2010.

For

Ed Foster

*You are experiencing
a minor distress.*

—Seyhan Erözçelik

EARTH SHADOW

Flat out
in the dark

I heard, above me,
some other guest say:

well, he had
a good run of it.

But seated at
my table

was a doctor.
He crouched down

and brought me
back to life.

Later,
test after

test found no
real reason why

3

*I died that
night.*

*I took a sip
of water.*

*I swallowed
as I stood up*

*and my heart
stopped.*

Iceland

Would this
     enshrouding

were the
emancipation of

matter, would this flame
were   of the

spirit, this
volcano

ethereal, guttering
forth from

a paradise of
white ice.

    *

Would the sky
mirrored the

earth, and in fact it does,
alive, now, with swirl of dirt, dark

smoke crossing
the ocean

in sulfurous
continents, ash

falling,   would
all places

were part of
an unfolding

cosmos
of

charcoal
      flakes.

*

Would
the upward

rush were angelic.
Would souls were assembled on

a mountain in
Iceland

begging to
utterly fly up,

to and through
the gate of a higher

and final
                fire.

Would
there were

a new body
for each.

              *

Would
that were

what you, too,
wanted, though you'd be

crushed, be dev-
astated,

when
all that

comes again, comes
again, but there is still the

joy of
that flight,

that ascent,
that forgetting, that

forgiveness,
which you

crave, have,
in your

way circled
the earth

in search of,
        that miracle,

that liberation, that
escape, up

through the
opening blown

in the sky,
where

the purified go,
where you are

not
just ash,

filthy, and
guilty, and adrift.

San Juan Islands

The mountain beyond is
a pure luminous sea of cloud

above a coiling blue plateau.
A part of the far coast is erased,

or is just a faint pencil line
under a chalky streak.

Whatever islands these are,
in whatever ocean this is,

this expanse of glowing blue,
one part smoother than any other,

they reflect the sky that reflects the water.
To the north, a diffusion of white,

clouds on the water like
snow on the mountain

and the blue, abiding
in the mountain's stone,

as if stone kept the color of
the sea it once rose out of.

Horizons of stone, cloud, trees,
the shadow of islands on the water

seems like a part of the islands,
or like snowfields of cloud

between some islands.
The clouds create a bay

that rests above the islands.
Some of the islands are clouds

or are floating on a cloud,
black on the white,

a touch of the sun's gold
on the low white waves of a veil.

*

These may be the islands
where the stones glow at night.

These may be the islands
where a lost girl with tangled hair

and a shell in her hand can see
the other side of the world.

These may be the islands
that drift away like a boat.

These may be the islands
about to sink below the water.

These may be the islands
where our fate is sealed,

sky pink behind the trees
until mist draws in the land.

(Tomorrow they won't be there.
They will never have existed.)

These may be the islands
that are only an outcropping

of rock in a blue magnitude.
These may be the islands

hidden by the other islands,
while to the south, to the

west: it's total ocean.
These may be the islands

of the madroña tree,
the red wood a cross of blood

in the bank of evergreen
bristling above the rocks.

These may be the islands
of the wings of a dragonfly

poised blue above a leaf,
islands of hornets, wasps, and bees.

There are nests in the ground.
The bees rise up like a cloud.

Their fire would cover
your face and arms.

These may be the islands
with troves of honey

in the trees, pits of honey
in the meadow beyond which

a lake of white light rests
on the water in front of

a dark grey island. The land
has snapped. There is a notch,

a gap, through which a dark
island can be seen, that may be

from where last night's
dream came, terrifying

and tragic. No one
should ever have it.

One's glad to wake up alive
in a tent on a bluff over an inlet.

The water is now
brighter than the sky.

Black scratches in lavender.
Are we heading toward

a continent, an open sea,
a platform of stone in the roiling,

visible only at low tide,
where a nineteenth-century fantast

stages pranks for voyagers:
a beautiful ingénue is

dressed up as a mermaid,
a surgeon in a white coat

pulls a string of sausages
from the body of a patient,

four men play cards at a table,
a barber, a pole, a chair, a client

his hair long strands of kelp?
These may be the islands

appearing in a sea of pearl,
of pale violet and silver.

It may be these islands are
crowns of a sunken continent,

as if exiles were always banished
in sight of an ancestral coast

that itself was in sight of
an island where the creator

set down the first man.
These may be the islands

where above us is a star
responsible for all radiance,

and for black, charcoal, grey,
violet, pearl, aqua, turquoise, teal,

all the colors that are
older than continents.

These may be the islands
from which tunnels run

deep through the earth and
end in the lands of the Hopi,

tunnels thought to be
9,000 years old.

These may be the islands
where the chief said

the tribe arrived from a star.
They climbed down ropes

made of celestial roots.
After the descent, and

possibly to their dismay,
the ropes became waterfalls.

the temple of Aphrodite

A Krakatoa
        yet to occur,

or a killer comet un-
detectable until

the day
    a telescope

loops Venus,
as if the atmosphere of

the earth were
the roof of

a ruin:
        in flames

—temple, twilight
orange bathes

                    the beams,
there is no inside

to the sacred
anymore,

only steps, arches,
a final sunlight,

and snapshots,
many,

of our bluish-
grey life . . .

        *

And trees, black, far
off, empty roads

curving upward, low
hills, forest, a glow

sunk in Love's
ruins.—This is

life without you,
goddess, holy

places obliterated,
a doorway, darkness

around it, steps
running up to

what no longer is,
in Turkey, Mexico,

Japan, Mississippi.
What remains is

a broken climb to
an exploded place

where even so
demonstrably

dissolute an
aspirant

as might
yet be you

feels a flicker
as a tabernacle

turns to a grey
empty void

in which these
stairs catch light.

*

No one else
seems to be here.

*

Have all been called
to the top step?

*

Have all been invited
to vanish from this,

the first place where
Aeneas fell asleep

after fleeing,
dreaming that

the orange on pillars
and groves is not the sun

but the pyre of
Dido, a last

glow reaching
(how could he even

begin to fathom it,
Baptist porticoes

in Mississippi,
monk huts

in Kyoto) all
stairs all around

the world that
just stop, mid-step,

blown away.
Any burned height

is a temple to
Aphrodite:

*

"upper
arms close to

her body, hands
extended, the hori-

zontal zones of
garment

filled with
a complex

figural relief:
Selene, Helios, Erotes—

the graces are
there,

so too is
Aphrodite,

not in local guise,
but half nude,

and on
a sea-goat,

with dolphins
leaping

at her side,
a divinity of

earth, heaven,
and sea."

*

For a time, all
icons of love

came from this city.
(An earthquake toppled it.)

Even before the Greeks
"the womb from

which all emerged"
found itself joyously

worshipped here.
And long after newer

gods stepped through
these ruins, hot springs

called the sick
from their beds

to bathe and heal
and so, coincidentally,

by Love's shrine,
a wide necropolis.

(Later, Mother of All,
your name is struck

from the stone, your
body toppled,

your vast matrix of
image making

becomes
Stavrapolis,

the city of
the cross.)

*

All pictures of
earth, of sea, and

sky show signs of
Aphrodite; any place

can become, for some,
momentarily, her temple,

at least by the orange light
of a fantastic sunset

or when remembering,
after many decades,

schoolyard loves,
their voices floating

over the nun's hedge
from the other side of

the convent, across
the girl's playground

as if blowing down from
the sky or across an ocean,

they seemed both close
and farther than Eurasia.

Then the perils of a note
passing through many hands

before it gets to the one,
folded and unfolded

many times along the way.
And if a note came back,

you pored over every word,
dazzled, ashamed, useless

for whatever subject
you were in the midst of.

Perhaps now you should
unfold that long-lost note,

at the top of a stair, where
a door once obscured a violet

sky aglow with pink,
and say aloud:

"Goddess, today
is my birthday.

I stand instructed in
the lessons no creature

does not learn. I
praise your powers,

you who protect and
punish all, perfecting

us in our hap-
hazard worship

as these stones are
perfected, quarried,

hauled, carved, hoisted,
(now scattered around a field)

to raise the temple
that still stands,

semi-transparent,
in whatever this light is

that seems somewhat other
than a copy of the sun."

after a painting by Randy Hayes

to Aphrodite

What is
   beautiful

      appears
   bliss-

ful in
   itself . . .

      *

So you, who are
called far-shining

in your emergence above
the horizon. Your

touch makes
the world

perceptible. (Though
Terror and Fear

are your
children.)

    *

You preside over
the "sensate particularity"

of creation, and
so, over every

shape in the world.
Without you, all would

be just particles
and force.

    *

The hours
welcome you.

They dress you
in ambrosial robes.

*

(In Delphi, it's true,
you were seen as

a goddess of death.
How startling

to spot your face
on a tomb.)

*

The art of
adornment

is the
only art.

A head is banded
in black, to blot

light from
the eyes.

*

(The psychiatric
term for this

is "complex
grief.")

*

Even at noon,
the time is always

night, a night spent looking
at photos of the sun.

*

The air awakens
to what is, to

whispers in a
prison:

the senses,
then, will not be

needed. Each skull
will feel

the breeze
for itself.

*

Someone steps out.
Lives go by.

A door is
closing.

*

(Drift, mind,
a million miles

from this
mouth.)

    *

Above bare trees
the moon is

a Gulag,
white

and
radiant . . .

at the gate

Dawn drops
into the pine grove, into

the prison
of

impossible
ideals.

*

Say God's
your lover.

Could even *that* so
bring the soul

to this edge of the senses,
especially during

a delightful
summer rain?

*

Deer float through
the trees and into a mist.

*

The village is
        astonished.

From deep
inside

the house
the sound of

her father's
grieving

reaches
those

gathering
at the gate.

*

(There is
only ever the

now
—and

the not-
now.)

A wave of blue
rolls through.

The grey overhead
turns a beautiful whitish

grey, as if the sky were
now the inside of

a cloud, or a
mountain range

beneath
the ocean.

*

(There is
only ever the

now
—and

the not-
now.)

after a storm

The shadows
        on the grass

are a beauty beyond
        fruitfulness.

No tree does
        not hold

some torn
        limb.

dream

A new life
as a small tangle of

shadows
amid a heap

of shadows, of spiders
in an empty house,

a spider among
spiders,

a dream where
it is the living who,

enduring
a death,

come back in new form, come
back, in this instance,

in a moving
tangle of

shadows
at the far end of,

far from the door of
a dark and almost

empty house
no place you

ever remember
living, yet

that woman
leaning in,

for a moment,
in profile, though so

much younger in the
light at the door,

must be your
mother

checking the
table for mail.

Must be, the
joy of seeing her

is so great,
who else

could it be,
saying,

no one's home
to whoever is

there,
outside.

the origin of fireworks

Where are the
fireworks

exploding this evil
night, this black dragon

feasting on my heart
as, once, upon that

of the Emperor
Li Shimin,

who, less alone than I,
and in an immense and

glorious palace,
commanded

the royal alchemist,
Li Tian, to drive

the sky monster back
through some novel

hole in the dark,
blown wide

with copper,
barium, magnesium,

and sodium
eruptions

(and for sparkle,
titanium), with

powders packed tight, lit,
arcing towards heaven

in a bamboo
tube?

　　*

In this long night
of no horizons,

will any
counselor

come, come close
and whisper

to me: *I have rockets*
to drive away

the beast
in the night sky,

the terror
biting

down into
    your heart.

A tabernacle is
so painted as

to appear in flames,
so that a door in the flame

would open, a scroll be lifted out,
as if the scroll came from

the flame, or was
written by the flame,

only to be, once
unrolled and read,

set back into the flame,
the rage of the flames

continually
scripting anew

the multitude of
letters flowing so

beautifully across
the scroll, the Torah

of flame in the moment of
its telling, with one

recurrent truth
amid all the laws,

dreams, genealogies,
and legends:

History is ashes,
prophecy is ashes.

     *

There is
only ever the

now,
—and

the not-
now.

flame tree

But when
Iris

recited her lines
about the flame trees in Africa

your mind was full
of flame trees,

of wonder and curiosity
about flame trees,

so that when, later,
in a hallway,

you saw her dressed
for a dance, you

were so
envious of

her escort, you almost confessed
what might, now, decades later, have kept her

from your
dream,

as if you knew right then that
years

in the future
she would appear to you,

so beautiful, in a formal black dress,
so elegant, as might be seen

at a concert,
at an opening,

though on her cheek,
a small cut, a gash,

a red cusp under
the bone.

    *

—I would love to catch up,
she says, but first immense distances

must be crossed, and
rather quickly,

oceans and mountains.
There will be more time to talk

as soon as we get
to a continent

beyond
even that Africa

where, as you might
remember

I once lived as
the daughter of a botanist

at the University
of the Dreaming Mind

there, doing
research . . .

*

The two of you set out,
you, even in your

astonishment
that she has found you,

that her beauty, her wound, and her words
so compel your assent

secretly hoping
you might, in

your passage, finally
see a flame tree,

that the hurry, the urgency
so evident in her tone

might nonetheless
require, along the way,

a moment of rest
perhaps

in the shadow of
a flame tree,

—if, in their cool burning,
they have shadows.

*

A death
bears down.

Her fear passes
into you, through you,

a fear so much more profound
than your own, your own

petty fretting
that,

in the panic of
this exodus

you may slip
past a flame tree,

its flowers of cold flickering
as astonishing

as Africa,
and not notice, and

Iris is too
distracted, by

the encroaching
calamity, too

absorbed in finding the way
to the waiting world,

to point one
out.

*

(To be fair,
those years ago,

she never said much
about her past, about Africa, about

her life there, though
her poetry did,

so vivid,
so secretive,

so utterly exact.)
Now, the dream decrees, you

will both be flying beneath the earth,
and through the earth,

to evade
violent spirits.

As in most dreams, much will
never be revealed. But

this is sure: All
aspects of

this adventure
came to be

through Iris, the world, the
rescue from it, the place that needs

to be reached: it is
all called forth by

her presence.
And you, who have long

believed in pretty
much nothing,

now espouse
whatever lets you sink

with her, deeper and deeper,
into, and through,

emerging—on what other side of where?—
in what may turn out to be

some blissful and
immaterial

body, now
accept

whatever truth lets you follow her, fly beside her,
whatever the fate of this escape,

to be with her forever,
with Iris, if only she would

turn her face
to you, though,

even
long ago,

her glance was
always so fleeting . . .

blossoms

As if they,
those nearly dead

leaves, were
once

or might yet be
in some unworldly

oncoming
season,

actual
blossoms.

    *

This pre-dawn
delusion was

enhanced, you might insist, by the noticeably
increased birdsong, so that along

with the thought
that blossoms blessed

a far away branch, came
the thought of

what
thought

the blossoms
themselves might

be, might be
thought to be . . .

*

If not yet now
soon or forever be . . .

*

And the thought
that within

the thought of
what the blossoms might

be thought to be
might be the heart of thought, of

the thought that
brought

them to be, like
the petals within the furl

of the first buds on a far away branch
in a heart where spring is

no longer
unimaginable.

    *

Brought
all these and

all everywhere to be.
Let's review: the thought of blossoms

and then the thought
brought forth

by blossoms,
and then

the thought that
brought the blossoms forth.

*

By the
apparition of

petals, by the contemplation of
the apparition of petals,

by the surprise of light
on a dark morning,

by the glow wherein you did not
know what you were seeing

thinking you saw
blossoms

that were in fact
dead leaves,

by the dead leaves
and the season of sorrow

and death
by a far-away tree

in a dreamless
winter

by the song
of returning birds.

    *

(The sun comes up.
The birds fall silent.)

    *

The tree is more
truly seen, the one tree

glowing amid the grays and browns,
glowing, not with blossoms,

but dead leaves
full of light.

    *

(The sun comes up.
The birds fall silent.)

*

The tree is more
truly seen, the birds are more

deeply heard,
their awe of

the thought of
the moment

when blossoms will be
of the miracle of the morning

that is
coming.

*

When blossoms
will be

there, in the dark
will no longer be a thought of,

a thought of a thought
of a thought

but seen,
there, on

some branch,
be thought itself

in the failing dark,
birds singing.

    *

The thought that brought
blossoms to be

will be known,
will show itself,

the way the blossoms
on the branch

show themselves, their light
waking me in the dark, in the deep dark,

in the death of
the season of death,

my dreamless
unrest

before daylight, the world
too quiet for any bird,

the thought that
brought

blossoms to be
will find me, be known

to me, deep in a dead
forest, before the

birds begin
and night dies.

    *

How long a sleep
is this world of

seasons, of sensations,
of light and dark, of so much

dreamless unrest, where,
while awaiting

nothing so
grand

as a hint or signal
of some celestial message,

we lie down
and forget what

ever might have
been said

to be securely known
before, that is, the birds sang

and I awoke
in failing dark,

I must have already
thought of

blossoms,
been thinking of

blossoms filling
my head,

as they are
about to

fill the world,
the wood, the night of

sensations, the thought of the
smell of

the blossoms, the
pure petals, pale yellow

and white and
pink

and the spray of light green
the thought of all these, amid

the grays and browns
and the thought

that brought
all these to be, that

woke me, that must have
been what

woke me,
before

I thought I saw
the first of what will be, here,

soon, the cascading multitudes of
blossoms, throughout the forest, before the thought of

blossoms
in dreamless unrest

before ever the
thought of

blossoms,
that

they were there,
had arrived, that in the course of a

single night, they
became visible,

and shone
forth.

earth's shadow

Where light fills airborne snow and water,
the aerosols in the eastern sky

can be illuminated in the
same way, red light scattering

on the border of
the shadow earth casts

on its own atmosphere,
a dark blue or grayish blue streak

along the horizon
opposite to sunset

or sunrise, most notable
at the anti-solar point.

At sunrise, earth's shadow
sets as the sun rises.

At sunset, earth's shadow
rises as the sun sets just below

the anti-twilight arch,
the belt of Venus visible

either after the vision drops
or before it again comes to be,

appearing pink with
backscattered red light.

Eventually both
earth's shadow and

the belt of Venus dissolve
in the dark of the night sky

though earth's shadow
spills hundreds of thousands

of miles into space, so that
sometimes the shadow

falls on the moon
and blots it out,

though the moon may retain
beyond the bare trees

a copper color,
or take the shade of

an apricot
amid ashes.

The shadow rises
faster than the sun sets.

The human eye cannot keep pace
with the sky as it darkens.

Daylight dulls us
but at sunrise

our night vision is acute,
not missing the least flicker

unless, that is, a plume of
sulphuric acid rises

from El Chichón
or Mt. Pinatubo

and the sky becomes
overtly fantastic,

even over once sacred
Athens, which Pindar called,

in fragment 64, the "city
of the violet crown."

DALLAS

If one had been born here
How could one believe it?

—George Oppen

Two small sons
who might otherwise

be dreaming are
alert to the first hint of

the limits of
    embodiment

flat on their backs,
kicking at the safety gate

across the door of
their room,

screaming,
and laughing.

    *

(Fifty years later
their ruckus

and revolt, their insight
comes back: "We're

lions! Lions!
Open the cage!")

*

Having already
in the course of their encagement

crayoned, over all the
walls, a jungle of

frantic, dazzling foliage and
coils of black briar.

And soon, in days to come,
they will pull out drawers which,

once emptied,
will become boats in

a big storm. The waves
will be towering

and ocean pour in.
Commands, calls for help,

the delight of pure destruction
will fill the down time

and the moment
draws close

when the boats
smash into

the reef of the wall
one after the other

and crack, and
break apart.

    *

        These idylls, these
            naps never to be . . .

    *

And at the other end of the hall,
closed door, in a nightgown

mid-afternoon,
exhausted, in bed,

at times, in tears
the mother

a stressed-out woman in her thirties
too beat to move, a record

might be playing, a radio on,
she might be mentioning

again what her
bachelor brother

once promised to lend her
when he's off in Utah

leasing oil fields,
a getaway, a "pad"

with a pool, a lake isle,
in twilight, peace

comes dripping
slow.

*

"You can come too,
if you're quiet.

You can even
go swimming . . ."

her firstborn, beside
her on the bed,

brushing out
her coif.

*

Brushing, gently,
caught up, throughout

the fraternal din,
in her talk or in music,

a symphony, a chorale,
or in her talk about

music, she softly
exulting in the

majesty, in the
soaring of others,

having lost her voice,
her singing voice,

from grief, her pure
tone, gone, now, months,

years, since her
father died, she is

unable to sing,
even a ditty,

even "Down by the
Salley Gardens."

At the end of
the nineteenth century

the world's center
was revealed to be Vienna,

its art and music
and intellectual culture

and above all
its most famous

address
Berggasse 19

where what most
troubled the world at

the beginning of
modernity

was also
revealed

and named
Hysteria.

*

At the start of
the twentieth century,

the world's center
drifted over to Zurich,

where through dreams,
drawings, and reports

from asylums
amid mountains,

the misery of
the new century

was researched,
studied in the context

of all places and
all times

and called
Schizophrenia.

*

After World War II
the world's center

left Europe. Given
the cataclysm of events and

the massive reordering of
social life it was

unclear when
the world's

center would
announce itself

or if it would be
Moscow, Peking, DC

(though it seemed clear
the new ruling

principle of
the age

would be
Paranoia).

*

In the latter half
of the twentieth century,

of what would come to be called
the American Century,

slowly, throughout the years of
sharp accelerations

in politics, technology,
sexual mores,

throughout the years of
the death throes

of long established
belief systems,

throughout the years of
the heroic struggle for corporate

sovereignty,
years of

worldwide revolts and repressions
in Africa and South America

and the Middle East
new flags, new capitols,

new cuisines
on our tables,

throughout the years of
doubt about the meaning

of style, crises about
cultural forms,

the world's center
revealed itself to be,

to have been,
where none had

predicted:
Dallas.

    *

And the affliction
deduced there,

deduced from the life itself,
deduced from the life of fossil fuels,

from the luxuries of oil
black as the sky,

black as the influence of
the darkening stars

that ruled the
postwar

night sky of
your earliest

years, if not of
your

nativity
itself,

was unveiled, there,
and given a

name,
Depression.

first memory

The beyond is
right there, right

on the other side of
that stretch of imperturbable

stones or bricks seen
once, through a window

in a strange house
sometime during

your first years
establishes, if only

now, decades later
the immediacy of

that expanse that is,
for you, the beginning

and the goal of
all thought,

the edge of
the unseen

the evidence of
all that is withheld

there, in the mind,
that recalled

wall, that
sunlit limit,

grass rustling
yellow against red.

August, 1959

Residual joy of the day
the nation gained a state

a state in pieces, the state
furthermost and afloat,

those islands of trapped ships
and billowing smoke

and bombed hospitals
flames from Pearl Harbor

still flickering, so it seemed,
amid the vast waste of the Pacific.

Above so deep a deep how
those scattered dabs

could never be the peaks
of undersea mountains.

Certainly they were moored,
somehow, to the sea floor.

This was the advent,
for you, of historical time.

The West Coast seemed happy,
less unguarded and alone that day.

Far out in the surging sea,
a new final outpost,

to observe the Japanese,
where visitors could feast

on pineapples, could watch
lava pour into the sea,

could hear, in the dwindling
sizzle between breaking waves

the great chains that held
the islands in place,

plunging rustling
chains, each car-sized

link dropping through
pale green where sunlight

still pierced the sea
until the light stopped,

in the cold silence,
in the deep wet dark.

Western Interior Seaway

For those born here
nothing is so fantastic

as the ocean, because all is
already floating, here,

upside down on
the depth of the sky,

the endless presence
of which over what was

after all formed by
vanished waters

is like a mirror showing
only what was or will be,

as if all that now is
land mass, roads,

architecture, in fact all
physical and mental

form, as if the present is
just debris floating upside

down on the cloudless
perpetuity of the sky.

Sky King

Through such a cope
flew, each week, a sheriff

in a small plane and
a big Texas hat

who tracked robbers,
rustlers, and lost children.

Whatever mayhem
was happening,

each episode of *Sky King*
took pains to replay

a version of the
same moment:

Word of misdoing
reaches Sky King.

He grabs hat and gun
and heads to the plane.

What needed to be seen:
more than the landing,

the mystery solved,
the conflict overcome,

the transgressors
brought to heel, the

parted reunited, the
spy revealed,

the reign of justice
reestablished on the earth,

the propellers roaring,
the dust kicked up,

more than the sky
or the king, the plane,

the "Songbird" rising
from the ranch runway,

banking always at the end
toward a wall of clouds.

The underside of
each wing gleamed

with royal insignia.
The show was in

black and white,
but in memory

the crowns
are gold.

October, 1962

Less the fret
over upcoming

world's end than
the thrill of new gadgets

—a transistor radio
and a huge flashlight,

tested then put up on
the emergency shelf—

is what comes back
from October, 1962,

the week some say
the sixties began,

the week of
missile intrigue.

The flashlight was
a gun pumped

with slugs of white,
the radio, fantastic,

small and green with
dials and antenna,

not to be touched
until the broadcasts of

those black arcs of
a promised oblivion

conjectured trajectories
linking Dallas and Cuba

had faded from
the evening news.

When the radio came
down, it was, ultimately,

a disappointment,
that first sample of

popular music
an irritation

to choirboy ears,
"Monster Mash,

a graveyard smash."
Or, "He's a rebel,

he'll never be
any good."

October, 1962

Less what is
than what seems.

Less the worry and the Civil
Defense announcements

than the radioactive
flourish of fallout.

Less a word so beautiful
the referent must be

spectacular, than snow,
heard of, but never yet seen,

white drifts in the yard of
the yet to be visited

ancestral land of
Massachusetts.

Less the petals falling
out in front of the house

from a pear tree,
or a magnolia tree

than manna falling to
the Israelites wandering

hungry in the desert,
following a flame.

At daybreak manna
gleamed on the sand.

It would taste like honey,
like morsels of warm

bread smeared
with honey.

Matthew 28:20

In later years she
would tell you about

Saint Teresa of Avila,
the inner castle, the joy

of the soul when free of
the materialism of this life.

And once, she spoke of
deep unhappiness

back in Dallas, when you
were young, before

the family moved back
to the north, before

the assassination
suggested the time

might not be right
for Catholics from the

northeast to feel at home
in the Lone Star State.

There was, apparently,
a dispute. This in and of

itself was revelation.
It was night. She fled

the house, fled to church.
The church was open,

candlelit, and empty.
Behind the altar, a risen

Christ looming within
a shimmer of gold,

a king seated between
the Alpha and the Omega.

One hand held the world.
With the other he raised

a pierced palm to all,
as when, on the last day,

he will wave away
the impenitent with

the deep red gash that
so astonishes the angels.

These wounds are, to him,
his ornament, his royal jewels,

his fair array. He will
be wearing them when

we are in heaven,
in the event the marks of

our own passion may
not be so visible upon us.

He will keep our deaths before us
even as we wait to celebrate

the wedding of the Lamb
and the nuptial night.

Your mother would say
later, in hushed tones,

in a dark hallway,
she was lost in her life,

confiding, late one night
what some might call

a nervous breakdown
but she spoke of as

a spiritual crisis, a trial,
praying and weeping that

one night, alone in the church,
while inside her head

words took shape, words
from scripture; inside

her, a voice spoke,
a voice said, a voice

said, to your mother
in all her turbulence,

a voice promised what
she rarely ever again

mentioned. Even unto,
the voice said. I will be

with you always,
even unto the . . .

This book is
an apocalyptic

theology of Dallas;
the following chapter will

address number mysticism,
what happens if nothing

happens, and when
the soul returns

to a street last seen
fifty years ago

and stares, furtive
and bewildered,

into a house given
over to strangers.

＊

(In an attempt to
answer the question:

Does such a visit qualify
as a haunting if

no one is
home?)

＊

At the window, peering in,
astonished: that simple cubes

of space still exist, as does
the bay window, where

back at life's beginning
you would often stretch out

on languid afternoons
in the square of light on

the blue carpet, feeling
the heat through the glass,

afloat in your body, drifting
in thought between the

warmth of the glass and
the blaze of carpet in currents of cool air,

thinking about the girl
across the street with

hair so blonde that
when out in her front

yard she stepped from
under the shade trees into

the sun her hair seemed
almost white.

*

The plum, pear, pecan,
and fig trees are all gone.

Only the magnolia with
its immense indolent petals

still looms, in the shade
by the porch, while in

the shadows of the living room,
it seems the duress of

second grade continues.
Your mother sits on the sofa

beside you and looks over
the night's homework. It is

about learning to carry
numbers, by way of

an abacus. The others
all know how to use an

abacus but you're new.
Math class is humiliating.

The abacus is like a toy,
with all its columns of beads

like a rattle, a horrible,
hellish little rattle.

(It's bedtime. Home-
work's not done.)

*

Beads of dread, green,
red, blue, like the dread of

prayers to be learned by heart,
in answers to theological

quizzes, even in the sheet
music assigned for choir

practice up in the loft
after dinner, evenings

with the stern German
choirmaster and his paddle.

*

But on the far left, those beads
were for sums too great

to work out in class.
Apparently purposeless,

these beads intrigued you.
Just to think about them

was eerie. They seemed
almost inter-galactic.

＊

(As if you could feel,
through the glow

of those aqua
colored beads,

the incalculable,
the infinite.)

November, 1963

No living soul
in Dallas does not

pass through Dealey Plaza.
And there is no part of Dallas

that is not a part of
            Dealey Plaza

of slope, overpass,
book depository,

that "elegant structure"
from 1901, rebuilt after a lightning strike.

There could never be
a Dallas without

a Dealey Plaza, just as
there could never be an Egypt

without the great gates
to immortality,

gates entered by
the sun each night

in his motorcade through
the twelve hours of judgment when

some are consigned
to the Place of Annihilation

and some to fields of bliss
to gather ears of grain

sheltered
by the feather of Ma'at,

the sun hidden
in the dark

in procession
towards rebirth.

Perhaps towards the
ruins of a razed Masonic temple

in Dealey Plaza
the killing of the king

has won approval
in the lodges;

apparently
this was needed,

apparently there was
simply no other way

to assure access to
the Space Program, to place

Masons on the moon.
A mystical method spelled it out:

Kennedy is Gaelic for
"wounded head."

The Queen of Beasts
Bovier, who herds the oxen,

arriving
at Love is

a beauty to be
dipped in blood.

*

In *Report*, the artist
Bruce Conner sees

the ritual structure of the
Kennedy assassination

as akin to Iberian
tauromachy, the fiesta

of the nuptial bull.
(A later analyst

elucidates: "Having in-
furiated the beast with darts, the

bride and groom spot their
garments with blood.")

Oswald, the matador,
Kennedy, the bull,

Ruby, the matador
Oswald, the bull, a world

of meat and blood
and appliances.

On November 22nd
a bull is led into the ring.

Jackie, the matador,
her dress, the red cape.

The sword-blow
the escotada

the breathlessness
the bouquet.

＊

All this to praise
the new life of death.

＊

So, the world becomes Crete.
So, there are no streets that do not

run into streets that
run into streets

that lead to the street,
Elm Street, that pours forth

into the labyrinth of
Dealey Plaza.

In the new life of death
Preston Road still runs past

Christ the King Grammar School.
In the new life of death

a nun opened the door.
She said turn on the TV.

We watched the TV then
we turned off the TV.

We knelt and prayed.
In the new life of death

we sense what it
means to be

from a particular
place on the earth.

All who die,
die in Dealey Plaza,

pass back into the flame,
into the eternal nothingness

through the portal of
Dealey Plaza,

through a great
invisible gate

by the white X painted
on the road, by one of

three white Xs,
one for each shot,

down the slope to
the highway,

to the triple
overpass.

vocation

A paying job, brushing
her hair as she rested,

long brown hair, chestnut
hair, flooding down from her head

a penny a stroke, though
it's tough to tally

the account once
she gets talking,

gets remembering, the
tales of girlhood, far away,

in the icy realm of the north
most certainly, or so

it seems, now, in
the sudden flood of

the moment after
half a century, herself

brushing to a sinuous
pitch of luster, buffing

with her God-given
Irish unreality

the simplest long-
gone day, which

in the recounting
left you astonished.

Touches of gold and red
in her sunlit flowing,

she, face to the light of
the window, other sons

napping—at last—
each stroke

gently various
from the top of

the head, the temple,
from just behind the ear

mid afternoon, mother, son
leaves, sky, light shade,

heft of handle in hand
a penny a stroke

never collected
incalculable pay-out

fifty years past
the flurry of day's lull

past a momentary
pastime turned

a calling: Listen
to the music,

she'd say, look
at those trees (limbs

now dark, massive,
empty tomb, old home

seized by time, taken
by fate, say what you see,

say what what you
see makes you think.

See if you can say
how far thoughts

can go, those
clouds in the trees,

those shreds in the limbs,
what are they, really?),

swirling of her hair
over the pillow, the fray

of single hairs at the
outer edge of the surge

now and then a snag,
ouch!, scrape of bristle against

cotton, brush pressing
through the hair,

how complicated
a knot can be

tough (now) to tally, lost
in tidal talk, a Dickens tale told,

an old movie—had she seen,
was it possible, every

movie ever made
in the thirties, in the forties?

The cobwebs and hopes
and grief and cake

and the flames of
Miss Habersham—

life is like this
she would say, you'll see . . .

all Hollywood's molls
and milquetoasts,

cops, thieves and
politicos and priests,

Jimmy Cagney whimpering
on the way to the chair,

and the desolate
parting of Ronald

Colman and Jane Wyatt
and what life would be

were this now
Shangri-La . . .

At the bend in some tress
in the twist of some

daughterly lock
spooling out

she might be speaking
beyond her death,

as until her death
now, if not then, so

deep then in her grief,
in the torrential mimic of

his talk, her voice
in years to come

wily and blunt,
forefinger jabbing

when his spirit,
stepped into her,

her father came back
often, to speak of things

in all their
coarse vitality

and dazzling candor
as he would to a son so

she to us, a patriarch
redivivus his instruction,

a wave in the water
of her talk.

*

She dreamed him alive and
wheeled into surgery.

Years from the now of this past
he holds out his own liver,

pearled with cancers
to her, his sobbing

helpless daughter, he,
in a hospital gown

propped on one elbow on
the gurney saying

I can't help you anymore,
where I am now but

if you want to
you can help me . . .

＊

Brush, sweep lightly over the skull
in warm afternoon light.

Sweep through the ripple,
the glitter of thought

on this maternal telling of the world
brush, hold within yourself

conservatory tales—
some historical laggard

composer waking to the hell of
an unresolved seventh

struck by his wife to get him out of bed;
the misadventures of your sister

raven-haired chanteuse,
and the lost friend, so gifted, the

name brushed long ago
from her thought

into your own,
flowing back now

Dana Frazer Lordly, the
accompanist, there the same

years as Cecil Taylor,
but died drunk, forgotten.

Brush, let this be
a Dallas of pure dreaming,

let thoughts and feelings be
only waves within the waves of hair

be just intimations in the bristles,
be hints in hand, be a whisper

passing, now, into what
forgotten for years, uncoils.

All her talk about
the transfiguring

touch of art, about the call
of artists, martyrs, mystics,

Thérèse of the Little Flower
dead so young, a fever—

she didn't know her own
beloved father when he

entered the sick room.
Terrified, she cried out.

She thought the hat he
carried was a huge spider.

(Flowers fell from heaven
on the day she died.)

    *

Brush, glide fully down
as the stroke begins to catch.

Hurry the flow of hair,
the cascade, the cadence,

brown or chestnut or tawny
glints of red and gold in sunlight

spilling downward from
behind the ear that

listened with such
devotion to all song

tapering over the flatlands of the pillow,
the plateau of the pillow, the

tumble of hair over
the precipice of the pillow

pooling in the shadows
and gnarls of the coverlet.

And her voice has spilled,
down and away, away;

brush, I barely remember
the side of her face

as she spoke, closed
her eyes, was quiet

and music returned, some
symphony, chorale, aria,

a broadcast performance
away, away, away.

     *

All Dallas
is dissolving.

The center of the world,
of such a world as this was,

pours into the earth,
blows into the sky

perhaps to appear
elsewhere, in

Lagos, Istanbul,
Kuala Lumpur.

    *

Brush, are you broken now?
Brush, are you sunk in the Gulf?

Brush, are you seared, melted
pressed into new form?

Do you linger in a landfill
or are you still in the

hands of the living,
re-entering the stream

of some fabulous flowing?
Tell us, are you still in a dream

greater than the real
as when, fifty years ago,

you were held by a son
combing the hair of

his mother as she talked, as if
with each stroke he could

dip his hand
in a magic river?

FIELD OF BLOOD

dream

Regardless, you
have been entrusted

to build, at a distance of
about twenty yards,

a second cross,
facing the first,

and to do so in secret.
And even were you not

consecrated to anonymity
due to raw weather

there is no one to ask about
the method or meaning

of such a possibly
profane doubling.

Moreover, the one widely
believed to have built

the first cross, a janitor
living in a building

across the street,
has vanished. The

second cross must be,
the dream decrees,

as smooth as
a single piece of

cut stone, yet built from
stray rocks hauled from the

banks of the river,
the Hudson, that runs

along the far edge
of the park.

As discretely
as can be, given

the flare of your red
slicker, you claw the flow.

Beside you,
you only slowly

notice, half hidden
in his grey hood,

as close
to ghostly as

he can get, helping
you out, is an actor

you think you
recognize,

though he is
famous

quite precisely for
disappearing

into his
roles.

As if the weather map
had been slashed,

those streaks, the paths of
the tornadoes, as if the claws of

the raven of God raked
their way through

several southern states
so that all earthly possessions

might fly up into the air,
plucked back through

the momentary funnel
of the beginning.

*

Wind flips a leaf over.
Rain strikes the underside.

*

So Heaven touches the earth;
so the divine, the mortal.

*

So, too, the mortal
can touch the divine,

as when in the crush of the crowd
around Jesus as he went to a dying girl,

whose father had fallen at his feet
and begged him to visit,

a suppliant, desperate,
a woman who had been

bleeding for twelve years,
unclean, shunned, there,

it must be supposed,
in secret, at great peril,

brushed the Redeemer's hem,
and her cervical hemorrhaging

was healed. And Jesus felt
the power go out of him.

He felt brushed by the
mortality of the body

he had descended to, had
seized, had entered, had stolen,

casting out, whoever
("and the multitude of

the archons was disturbed").
With the touch of the suppliant

Jesus had a foretaste of
his upcoming agony,

of all that would, soon,
flow from him as well.

He began to wonder what
a wound might mean.

He began to fathom
what bleeding feels like.

*

Jesus fed multitudes.
He withered the fig tree.

He drove the devil into a swine.
He drove the swine off a cliff.

He called Peter, terrified,
out onto the waters.

In the days after his death,
after he returned and stood

before the apostles with
his scarred resurrection body,

the astonishments continued.
Jesus slipped through shape after shape.

He appeared to one as a child,
to another as an old man.

He cured leprosy, dropsy,
blindness, he brought great joy.

After he ascended to heaven
the apostles, too, cast spells.

They, too, healed the sick,
traveling the Mediterranean,

proving the power of
whom they spoke.

  *

Judas, by contrast, worked
only one real miracle,

but it was the one upon
which all others depended,

the one even Jesus could not
contrive, the only act of

magic that mattered.
Judas freed Jesus from

the body he had stolen,
from which he had exiled

the occupant, of whom
no mention is made,

the body soon to endure
a horrific death, legendarily

cruel (a death, though,
not much worse than many).

Judas loved his brother.
He performed the miracle

so clearly beyond
all other miracles:

the kiss on the cheek
in the garden at twilight,

the miracle of
betrayal.

Gethsemane

In
   the

world and, now,
about to be

of it, this
the

long
moment of

      becoming
        of.

   *

The moment of,
the hour

of, *of.* Of
leaving

the world,
the hour of

the town below
settling   into sleep.

*

Hour alone, hour
afraid,   long

hour of
agony,

of
in, of about

to be
of.

*

Torches,
the kiss.

The sword,
the sliced

ear. The
slave.

*

The trees
gasp.

*

          Hour of Gethsemane
          Hour of Paradise

Hour of the cry of
becoming of,

which is the cry of
asking it not to happen,

becoming is the
moment of

asking not to
become.

Let it not be
a request by a god

not to be, be
alone, be afraid

be murdered.
The trees cry out.

Not the trees,
the leaves.

The cry is in
and of the leaves.

A breeze cuts through
a grove of olive trees

at the hour
a god is

beginning
to be.

                    Hour of Gethsemane
                    Hour of Paradise

Turns out the cross will be
a cross of wood

not the cross of light
spoken of to the elect

perhaps at this hour
by an otherworldly Christ

in a secret cave high
above the Place of Skulls.

The wood that will be the cross
laments what it must do.

The hewn trunk
has its own agony,

even the axe in its arc,
the tearing apart of the trees,

the opening of the grain
of the wood to the air—

earth and sky have
their own agonies—

hour the ear of the slave
is struck by a sword,

sword of the apostle,
the ear of the slave

on the ground,
ear of the ground

hearing the dismay of the sky
or ear turned to the earth

hearing the roots,
the rocks, the layers

of sediment, the residue
of oceans and heat

torn off from a star
lift up their outrage,

their terror, hour of
blood pouring

from his head, blood
on the ground of the garden,

blood pouring from the side of
the head of the slave

who heard the
voice of the god,

standing so close to
Judas and to Jesus

even heard the kiss
on the cheek,

a kiss as light as
a rippling leaf.

Hour of Gethsemane
Hour of Paradise

To not stay awake
just one hour, at night,

to not keep vigil
when asked, to sleep

in a cold grove, to
drift, oblivious,

to dream in
a dark garden,

is yet to be a part of
what is coming.

   *

      (The faithless three
      sleep so that

      the hour of dreaming
      might be established.)

   *

Regardless, elsewhere,
under the olive trees,

a god begs not to
become of the world.

Regardless, it might
yet prove to be all you

have written is just
one dream among

many that first came
to these sleepers,

settled in the heads of
these dozing apostates.

Elsewhere, the cup.
Elsewhere, the sweat,

(hour alone, hour afraid)
while, in a cold grove,

each, awaking, will
remember nothing of

the will accomplished,
so that every dream

across the sleeping
earth after this heroic

moment of rest
in a dark garden,

every dreaming head,
in Christendom,

and beyond,
and after,

will be composed
of a mixture of

heaven
and death.

Hour of Gethsemane
Hour of Paradise

The birds in Gethsemane
don't know the sun is coming back.

By midnight they forget
that the day ever was.

All of existence is dark.
The world, it seems to them,

has never not been dark
so that every morning

is an immense surprise,
and this is what explains

birdsong at dawn, that outcry
of delight, bewilderment, and awe.

Nothing like this has
ever been seen before!

Were they human they would
cry out: God is glorious!

Soon of course will come
the rediscovery of flight,

what carries a song
can carry as well

the entirety of being,
but first the multitude

must recover their calm.
This can take a while,

the very while the world
takes to emerge from the dark

as shape, volume, density, distance
though the properties of light

exceed all those that
light makes visible.

This may be no conclusion
the birds can reach, at least

not in the excitement of song,
and not in the frenzy of their flights

across forest and field
so much of their day

simply not given over to
contemplative intensities.

And if the birds in Gethsemane
do not remember in

the depth of night the day
perhaps in its blaze,

they lose the slow
swallowing of the seen,

forget the hours when wings
are only a cloak against the cold,

after the hour of nightfall,
in the hour of stillness

when they see the world
go away and cannot conceive

what song is, no memory
then of having heard song

or of having sung, in that
eternity before dawn

during which there is
nothing to do but dream,

dream, in the dark, of day
not knowing what it is,

quiet in Gethsemane
but poised for joy at

the sudden coming to
be of the sky.

                    Hour of Gethsemane
                    Hour of Paradise

As when one wakes
to find oneself crucified,

upside down, but at an angle,
about forty-five degrees

perhaps so as not to
presume to be Saint Peter.

The cross is an X
stuck in the earth

at just one of its four points.
Upside down, hard to tell where,

you seem to be in Rome.
It's night in an empty parking lot

but the city is lit up
in front of you.

There is a dome,
spot-lit and white,

that could be the Vatican,
be DC, be any state capital.

You're wearing an old cloth raincoat.
Your head is oddly clear

despite all
the rushing blood

and, again, odd, no
pain in the extremities.

Not one sensation
indicating a nail

through your hands
or your feet

though your outstretched
arms stay in place

(your failing embrace
of the earth)

as do your legs held
to the upper V of the wood—

legs to the upper V
arms to the lower V—

head just hanging down,
disoriented but no real

sense of blood rushing
down the one edge of the letter

driven into the ground.
What does it mean,

to be crucified
on an X, a question

that in your relatively
painless state occurs,

but distantly, a matter
you intend to get back to . . .

There is no one around
just lights from traffic,

the base of numerous
trees, there must be

moonlight
or starlight,

there seems to be
no getting used to

the optical challenge
of the moment, to turn all

right side up
in your head.

It's painless, peaceful,
but puzzling as well,

to be crucified and
conscious through the night,

feeling sweat pour down
in such cool weather,

(though it could
be blood)

no sense of how
that happened

no sense at all of
what belief you might

be the startled
martyr of.

Perhaps crucified
is the wrong word.

What does one
call to be

put to death on an X?
It's like an old high school math

problem: what is
the meaning of X,

or is it: what is the
value of X?

Or is it:
what

would be
the

death of X,
the value of

the death
of X?

false positive

Jesus steps into hell.
Lids of coffins lift away.

    *

The souls of those long
lost are led closer to the light.

Whatever of it, that is,
they can grasp, the door,

shattered and to one side,
the banner, the blazing figure,

the new life so brightly
before them. Soon to be

in greater proximity
to the presence,

these lingerers in limbo,
the virtuous, born too soon,

the un-baptized, will
somewhat ascend.

*

When Jesus sweeps
down the day before his

return to life, the unborn
are there, the born dead are there;

so, too, those souls who
never passed through

the veil of fire, through
the hallway of the womb,

the parlors of birth
to the great gardens and

sorrows of this world,
the almost souls, that is, of

the never quite conceived, the close
but not quite, summoned

nonetheless into a form
of being by, after years

of trying, a false
positive, after years,

after, at first, uncertainty:
a conversation by the water

by the shimmer of a reflecting pool
in front of a war monument

on a romantic evening,
the question, tentative,

seemingly casual but quietly
overwhelming: children,

do you want them?
Do we both want them?

What if one of us wants
children, a child. What if

one of us wants one
and the other doesn't

not want one, could we
let one come to be, inside

one of us, inside, that is, that
would be, me, could that happen,

were I sometime to want that,
having thought long about

my feelings about where I came from,
all that, all that that was, all of

what brought me to be,
what can be grasped of it,

were I then to want that,
were you to not not want that,

could we bring about a birth?
Wait, wait, and then too late

is that all it was, would ever be,
we were too late, simply that,

the consultants, the clinics,
the unborn waiting to be,

the drugs, the procedures,
the years, the expenses, the cost,

nothing, nothing happening,
going broke and trying, in debt,

trying, then one day
late in the biological day,

the last biological sunrise
for the body I find myself to be,

came what seemed to be
the word, the joyous word,

the annunciation, when
for fifteen minutes,

a child was coming to me.
Science brought on an ecstasy

just this side of what
could be called bearable,

a child was coming, was inside me,
was about to be inside me.

   *

So souls are called into
being! Into, it turned out,

not the ranks of the living, but
those of the never-quite.

In the hierarchies of the
soul, is that a category,

the not-quite? Dante who
saw much, but did he miss this

when, in *The Divine Comedy*,
he said Jesus stepped into

upper hell to bring those
there closer to perfection,

were the never-quite
among them, the ghosts of

a hope for whose sake
so much seems possible

as we dumped our accounts
into the teeming coffers

of an endless series of highly
recommended fertility experts,

with the one act of intercession,
that fifteen minutes, a slight

chemical error whereby
I stepped into heaven,

whereby I cried, wild with joy,
I was pregnant, broke and

happy as a girl
from the mountains,

the ancestral mountains.
Dante, the never-quite have

a life, at least in the mind, in the mind of
a spectral mother. My child came

out of limbo, into life,
for fifteen minutes.

A mother. I was a mother,
for fifteen minutes.

I stepped out of limbo.
I stepped into heaven, not

believing that what is
not real is not real.

dream of the rood

A tree shines before you in a dream.
The dark of your sin is the shadow of the tree.

   *

On the branches, gems, like five live flames,
flames that pulse above the flowing of the wood.

   *

The branches are the world's uplifted arms.
Blood seeps from the bark on the trunk.

   *

Amid the dark of the blood of night's dream
the tree pours from the earth into the sky.

   *

A tree as wide as heaven itself, it has been said,
held together by invisible nails of the Spirit.

*

The world is a forest in deep winter.
The guilty dream, there, of the tree of all trees.

*

The tree that touches heaven, it has been said.
The tree that firms the earth with its roots, it has
    been said.

*

The tree that grasps all the space between
the two, it has been said, with immeasurable love.

*

O crucified, joy of the universe by which
dark death is destroyed and life returns to all.

*

(So, in the eighth century,
Boniface cut down a huge oak.

Diviners had often gathered there.
So Barbatus wasted a great tree

*

hung with the skins of beasts,
melting a gold viper down for a chalice.)

*

Your life is the dream of the trees' sleep.
Each dream is a dark branch that glitters.

*

The death of your god is itself a dream.
(Trees tend to speak at the turning of a world.)

*

That leaf or jewel under your pillow
is the seed of all prophetic dreams.

*

Each dream is a tree in a forest of jewels.
(Everything done to the god was done to the tree.)

*

A dream summons the dark you are.
Your dreams are trees that bleed and speak:

    *

I was pierced, lashed, mocked, cut,
my pain as great as if I were the god.

My wounds were not then the jewels
of the dream that bears to you, now,

one who merely held a body up to the sky,
who said nothing, who could not cry out.

My travail has never entered speech.
I am a span of speechless agony.

I would never commend my spirit,
never ask why so forsaken. I am

all that suffers without expression,
nails pierced me, pinned to my crown

a useless, fluttering scroll of words.
Once a tree in a forest of trees

slain on behalf of an unknown god
like the leaves you see as the green

drains into the shadows of your sin.
All life is death in the agony of

the tree I am, again, a jewel with wounds.
I was made a cross, a dreaming cross,

then a dream of a tree that came to you,
jeweled leaves on a bleeding tree

that find you in a northern forest,
deep in a guilty sleep. You yourself

are a dreaming cross, adorned,
a jeweled sword, bloodied for

the sake of one elaborate riddle
the riddle that all poetry voices

all poetry that would be true to
the Calvary each moment enacts:

I have five jeweled wounds,
I bleed from my side: what am I?

I mingle terror and love: what am I?
A ships' keel gone astray? What am I?

The world tree, on which Odin hung?
what am I? Sin is a riddle. Salvation

is a riddle. Sacrifice and the soul,
the riddles of a new god from the south.

The immense, relentless onslaught,
the seeming need for a body to bear it,

the humiliation, the spit, the cloak,
the falling down along the path,

the veil, the assistance, the betrayals,
the darkening of the afternoon sky,

the merciless sponge, the cry to
the father, the frenzy of cruel actions,

are rare riddles, when solved,
they merely increase your pain,

like a jewel-encrusted tree
in the opulence of autumn,

a dream of death, a dream in leaf,
in a world where all light is jeweled . . .

DARK CHURCH

Dreamstanbul

Two bits of
    spine are now

        blades. The blades
            nip a nerve.

   *

        "You are experiencing
        a minor distress."

   *

An agony, in fact,
searing neck, shoulder,

arm, hand, fingertips
impossible,

then, to lift up one's
head, even to

look over, over and down
to the never-seen

Aegean,
whatever

color it might be, one is
dreaming, in pain, it might be,

and Troy and the
Dardanelles

below the lowering
plane, unseen, because of . . .

    *

        "you are
          crossing seas"

    *

A sudden gap, a gasp,
a grip, between vertebrae,

by vertebrae,
of nerves

one feels betrayed,
stabbed in the back by the bones

in your back,
bent, hours,

gasping
arm aflame . . . ?

    *

       "The Aegean light
       doesn't let me see it."

    *

Weeks later, a friend
will spin a tale of

origin, to help you
clarify the damage: "In a

previous
life, you

lived in that
city, now Istanbul.

I believe
you

were be-
headed there . . ."

      *

           "Then, I died."
           "I won't *die* again."

      *

Otherwise
from glowing

water towers and hills
shoot up, masts and

sails in a blue blur,
in that city, that

kingdom of
domes, flags,

minarets,
archways,

stairs, altars,
battlements,

bewildering
letters, tiled

heavens shining
on high above

the upturned head of
whatever pilgrim

might arrive—circle of
saved faces

peering down
from within

the blossoming
rose of heaven.

*

"Dust is a mirage
inside the rose."

*

Otherwise,
there,

open to the sky,
in adoration, in awe,

but for this gnarl, this notch
cut in the core of the

spine at
the outset of

devotion, if only
to art, you

will see none of it,
see quite possibly

nothing
but, abed,

curled in the one
painless posture, should

luck let you
so settle,

the ceiling of
your hotel room.

    *

        "stinging nettles are
           blooming in my heart"

    *

Otherwise
waking

within
an image

at the center of
an image

of some lost
but still persisting

celestial totality,
regarding

which
casual but

contemporary
testimony

drifts
in:

    *

        ("I didn't think that
            place was much of

                anything, then I
                looked up.")

    *

Otherwise
at the lowest

point within
ungraspable being

the pearl the Prophet spoke of
would appear, a white

flash, there then
the radius, the circle,

the dome, the shimmering
air-borne sea of

tiles, light, shadows,
the plenitude of

the pure   '
present

engulfing
the honeycomb of

triangles that hitch the heavens
to the cube of

the earthly world,
itself rising to that ring of sky

that bequeaths all our
dimensionality,

there to be
seen in

the verticality
of the aleph,

the horizontal
whirl of the bey.

A hymn of
Koranic light

is pouring down
into petals of

vines, letters of
turquoise and cobalt

perfection, amid
pomegranates

pinecones,
veins, vines,

crystals, tulips
spirit reaching into

the timeless sphere,
into all our

polyhedrons, deep
into the cave of the world, of

appearances,
its vault

corresponding
to heaven, and its

piedroit
to the earth,

adorned with a
canopy of seashells

the shell, the ear of
the heart, would

receive divine
secrets,

place where
Sayyidatna Maryam

hid in
the temple

fed by angels
until "the pains of childbirth

drove her to the
trunk of

a palm-tree:
she cried out:

    *

        "Ah! would that I had
                died before this!

         Would that I had been a thing
              forgotten and out of sight!"

    *

                     of Sura 24

Otherwise
a niche

chest high in a wall
that amplifies the light of

a lamp.
The glowing

fills all space
the light from the oil

from a tree from a place
neither in

the East nor the West
a place, that is

neither
Christian nor

Jew,
light from

a lamp
in a niche

oil from a tree
deep in

Syria,
oil that

illumines
though

untouched by
fire, the glass in the

lamp is like
a star.

*

(Similitude,
likeness, metaphor,

this is how God
speaks   this is how

God leads, no, guides
us, by light

upon light, light over
light, light

through and
within light.)

*

Hotel Yesil Ev

Otherwise
your heart is off

to adore jeweled footstools
        in the treasury   of the Sultan.

Otherwise
your intellect is off

to worship
weapons

in the armory of the Janissaries
(and machine guns   at the Black Sea.)

    *

Otherwise
in a Roman

bath house your soul
lies naked, beneath a towel,

an attendant fingering warm
gels into her neck,

her shoulders, her
arms, her back.

She feels . . . what . . .
transported . . .

A warm wet cloth
        wraps her head.

  *

Otherwise,
you loll

amid pillows
as beside an urn in

Hagia
Sophia, in

shadows in
a dark corner apart

from
the probable

throng,
cupping your

head with your hand
and tilting your

eyes up, in
what

otherwise
might be

ecstasy.
Though not

quite cruciform
you are

like
a cathedral, in that

the altar, your head,
feels pried apart,

smashed,
torn out

by invaders
who, in awe of

the ring of eternity
shining

above, raise
the words

of the prophet
overhead,

set them at the
center of the cosmos

the calligraphic
whirl of . . .

*

Otherwise
were

these curtains
walls in the Blue Mosque

your arm might not go numb,
the arm and then the hand,

the hand that holds
this pen,

you might
well write out

the Creator's name
find ways to praise him,

praise the purity of the force
that moves all matter

yet stays so
still, fly

to heaven and back
in a single night, and look up,

look around,
might throughout

the immense flight study the
arc of

the sky, the celestial bodies,
the path to Paradise

and enter it, feel
your first

twinge
of eternal life.

＊

Otherwise,
restless in the

hotel calm you might
still feel, at varying angles, and with

unpredictable degrees of
force, the drift of a

dispassionate
blade, into, and

through, the grain of
your spine.

＊

Otherwise,
your heart would be

tiles set into a wall, each at
its own tilt,

light pulled in from
all the angles and sent out

hushed dark,
the gold glows.

Your intellect
shops for taffy, your

soul lies under ladles of
warmth, the soap foaming,

and you grow curious
how far

without
the intercession

of some holy force,
you can lift your right arm.

*

Otherwise,
                darkness.

All afloat in light,
domes, nested, and

over-
lapping.

Otherwise,
the ping of yet

to be quenched wine
glasses,   in their drift

from tray to table
a cluster of

pings
floating up

the stairway, up
from the

garden
of an

Ottoman
        extravagance

                turned hotel,
a clamor of

silverware,
a rustle

of table cloths
foretelling

    the night of
the

soul's
wedding.

As if
otherwise

      arriving
otherwise

        awakening
as if   after a long flight

came deep sleep
in a basement room

as if Istanbul
were Byzantium

were Constantinople,
were,   could yet be,

Dream-
   stanbul

as if   were it not for
the sine wave of empires

not for the transformations of
science, this room

might still be
the birthplace of

emperors,
a door into the world

for descendants of
Constantine.

Might be,
might yet be

were all, at last, to be
otherwise

be, so that all
will be, finally,

otherwise,
the crib of

some definitive
ruler,

who will conquer by *in hoc*
what could only be

to us now
in this era enduring

the cessation of
revelation

a spectacularly
bewildering

if not unintelligible
                    signo vincet   as if

otherwise
        arriving

                    otherwise
                            awakening

as if   the light of what
morning finds you

awake in
a basement

a cheap room in
the old part of the city

looking closely at the walls,
the brick, the archway,

the floor, the ceiling
familiar from

books and maps
and artworks

and beginning to sense
exactly where in the city

late in the night
crossing oceans

you have arrived
where this room

now
is

and where it was,
centuries ago, what earthly

                    magnificence
                          rose up around it

from
              which to infer   if not

                          some new
                                birth

if not a rebirth at least
                          a ghost of one,

an intimation of
some glimmer

in the void between
epistemes, where you might

in your wanderings
now be, eyes wide

and dreaming, dreaming
that all might at

any moment be
otherwise

in Istanbul,
abed, in

a low lodging
once the nativity

chamber of
a great palace . . .

for Seyhan Erözçelik

Might be an isthmus
a place that bleeds two seas

whose sweet and bitter mixes
do not enter each other,

a place where
the greatest pearls

are to be found,
the *barzack*,

the place between
death and resurrection,

a place the master of
coffee grinds and

rose petals might see,
a place appearing

in the shape of dark grains
in the play of thorns

visible here as
from wherever you

otherwise are;
you see the future

you feel the present's
otherwise ever unfolding

ecstasy nothing
ever to be

mentioned in passing,
even in the beyond

with which
the world of

the living
craves ecstatic

union through an
excess of wine,

even more so
through the intoxication of

tears since
wine

costs money
but tears are free . . .

The Bosporus is
turning violet as has

the Golden Horn, as has
the Black Sea, hour in a bar on

a deck over the water,
hour in Europe,

hour in Asia,
hour a third place,

which unites and
divides them

both, Istanbul,
boats, flags, hour

too fully in the
throes of such a

"minor distress"
as you might have said

have been said
to prophesy

too delimited to
take up your offer

and come to your house
and sip from the cup

of Rumi and
Hafiz,

Cavafy and
Mandelstam,

sip wine if not
tears, cocktails if

not wine, sip oblivion if not
transcendence.

Next time, next
time, for sure, I'm

already there,
in a next life as in

a previous, all the while
here on the water as twilight

fills the edge of the
primordial Siberia

from which,
it is said,

your word
magic derives,

flooding from before
Islam into Islam

enflaming your feel
for the arc of the

plunge of
the soul,

the arc of
the escape, the great

truth of Turkish
Sufism. A cup to our lips

awakens us to
flames.

Stinging nettles are
        blooming in my heart

To such
paradoxes of

embodiment as that
you were let go

from the hospital
yet you are

still dying
even as

you invite me
over for some chat

though these were our final words
in this blaze of

the in-between,
of a drink

not with you
until a year

after your death
when back in the States, in that

other Istanbul,
Seattle,

the Seattle within
Seattle, the studio of

an artist, a picture,
the gist of some other

Turkish meander,
an outdoor café,

mid-afternoon,
those there having

each picked up
an ashtray,

dumped the ashes out
and wiped the glass clean.

Each holds an ashtray
to the sky and is

looking through it.
It would seem

the camera has captured
the birth of the lens,

an image of
the appearance of

an image within
the moment of

the miraculous, of
the moon swimming

across the sun, of
shadow falling across

the face of the earth,
of the air shining with

a bright darkness
all so that now

a new
intoxicant

clarifies creation,
citrus parings,

gin, and a spritz of
something else,

a "Turkish Eclipse,"
a martini dreamed up by

the artist to mark that moment
and sipped, now,

in deference to
all moments within

moments, all images of
light flying free

from a black core
—intrusive moon—

of the appearance of
night within the day

of immanence
within the beyond

of end as origin,
all images of

prophecy and
recollection

of rose petals,
as are to be found

in your poetry,
in such abundance

images within
your images—

like a death that
dissolves

within a
larger life.

Dust is a mirage
    inside the rose.

Ararat

Noah called to the people
by night and by day.

　　*

By night, that is, by
appeal to their

intellects and spirits.
And by day, that is, by

appeal to their
senses.

　　*

As the rain fell
Noah called, not

understanding the true
nature of such a call.

He gave the call by day
during the day, and

the call by night
during the night.

＊

So Noah failed, failed
to tell the world.

＊

Noah and his family
were not, therefore, saved.

＊

Of all the peoples of the earth
Noah and his family

were the only ones
not saved.

＊

Had Noah made the
call by night during the day

and made the call by
day during the night,

were such warnings possible
in that epoch before

the coming of
the Prophet

then during the day
the world would think of

the God of night,
the God beyond,

the incommensurate
God, and during

the night, the world would
think of the God of day,

the God whose law
is resemblance.

*

In denying the call by day
in the day those who

drowned affirmed in their
ecstasy the God of night.

In denying the call by night
in the night those who

drowned, whose cries
of ecstasy were lost

in the roar of the waters,
affirmed the God of day.

    *

Those who drowned were
not the corrupt and faithless.

    *

Those who drowned were
martyrs and Gnostics

swept off to paradise
in the waves of the One.

    *

At the sealing of
the entrance to the ark

at the focusing of the sky
at the quick drift of clouds

at the first of the ecstasy of the planet
at the *fana* of the fallen world

at the brimming of wells
at the satiety of the water table

at the spill into street
at the slide of hillsides

at the flow of mud
at the delight of fish

cruising new kingdoms
at the celebration of the deserts

made perfect by their long thirst
at the release of palaces

and barracks and hovels,
of all bricks back into

mud and straw
in a vast dissolve

at the sinking of
the last landmarks

trees, hills, mountains
monuments, shining walls

on top of mountains
at the purifying of the sky

at the craving of the birds
for the end of the effort at flight

for the last of the notes of their songs
to be lost in the stormy wind

and the bodies of livestock
the carcasses of pets

bequeathing themselves
to the zeal of the spirit

at crops now swayed one way
and then another by

currents across the floor of
the ultimate ocean

at the petals blown on a breeze of water
from quiet gardens, untended

at cups, toys, tools, jewels,
mementoes, weapons,

coins, clasps, baskets,
implements, ornaments

washed of all simple intent
at the opening of the beyond

at the onset of presence
at the deepening of depth

at the drenching of the intellect
at the suffusion of the heart

at the whirl of the waters
at the martyrs and Gnostics

lost in the love of
the paradox of God

during the day, during the night
for forty days and nights.

     *

dream

The house has been
purposely deserted

so you can gather what
you need and get out.

Marriage over, you
need to go elsewhere.

     *

(The feeling, on waking,
is that you are

about to be
dead,

and will not see your
sons again.)

*

A dew drop on a grass blade
will be the next flood.

*

Clear day, perfect sunlight.
An imperceptible torrent is falling.

*

Air is an ocean that overwhelms the earth.
Long after Noah, the world is still awash in majesty.

*

The sky pours down to the earth.
The earth is rising to the sky.

*

A dew drop on a grass blade
will be the next flood.

*

Who will call to us in the day
with the call by night calls to us

in the night with the call by day
so that the transcendent and

the immanent will
no longer be divided,

call with the call that
will say: all is like God

and, nothing
is like God.

    *

Call with the call that will tell you
you are burning

and drowning, and
you don't even know it.

You are drowning
in flames and

    *

don't even
know it

    *

in the flood of the flames of
the paradox of

God's
love.

Anatolia

Otherwise
might drop down

inward prophetic fire
otherwise, what pours through

an arm, numbness
across hand

might be otherwise
and the fingers, kindling

the fingers that hold the pen
invisibly burning

might write
"otherwise."

Anatolia

Nothing,
otherwise,

to be seen all this
downcast pilgrimage,

nothing but the
ground.

Goreme

Tombs and tunnels,
naves of the snake church,

Basilica of
St. Basil,

Basilica of the Apple
seen and entered, the dark church,

with its excavated sky
interim of ash, dim

fresco of
Gethsemane, haloed

Judas,
patriarchs

gathered to one side
in a hole in a hillside in a ravine

of monastic cells
in a crater of

contemplation
window in the ash,

dark light hole, dash of sky
over alcoves, arches,

pillars in the dark,
dark church, an earth

within the earth,
lie down, look up

brightly painted ash,
in dim light

inner lid of a
planetary casket,

alone, stretched out, eyes open,
petrified char inflamed by

betrayal, nearby,
depredated

incandescence
of a once

salvific
history.

The sky is now
below the earth.

Final angels in
scraped hollows.

Glint of apocalypse
on stilled lava.

Golgotha,
fresco'd.

Sky of Jerusalem,
earth of Cappadocia.

Dark church,
numinous

prayer
hole.

The sky is now
beneath the earth.

Downcast
Christ,

chin
on chest.

Hope is now
beneath the earth.

Sky of Jerusalem,
earth of Cappadocia.

Thirst. (Soon
will come:

I thirst.)
Dark church.

A mother is
given a son,

a son,
a mother.

Cappadocia

You could be beside
a stream and not know

that just beyond the brush
the stream runs on through

a garden as does a flood
of fish in the heart of

the flowing, and rising
from rocks at the midpoint

as if floating, are chairs,
a table laid out with silver,

a candlestick, a carafe
above the glittering rush.

The tablecloth flutters just
above the frothy flashes

while wailing along the bank
appears a beautiful woman,

black hair, yellow
dress with white trim.

A parasol shades her step.
In her other hand dangle

sandals by their straps.
She may soon prove to be

a companion for lunch just as
the stream may soon cut

through an orchard and spill
into wilds that run to the

mountains that rise
from this arid plateau

and ring the cave within
which is your hotel.

Her name is Julie. She
may tell you a dream

in which she sees the ghost
of her dead husband ride

a bicycle through the Alps.
She seems a bit lost.

By way of telling how
she has found herself

barefoot in a stream in
Cappadocia she may say:

"Earlier this morning
I went out for the mail

but the day was so
great I just kept going."

Pergamon

Walls once marble,
white but fiery

noted by ships at sea,
the glow of amphitheater,

barracks, and the gates
all walls touched,

torched by
the sun's gold

at sunset; hilltop
bastion, visible as well

as evening came on would
have been the now stolen

"Throne of Satan," by
which the Book of

Revelation
seems to mean

the great altar now
housed in Berlin.

Apparently aflame
were this truly

the second century and the
wall's wealth yet to be pillaged,

would as well be the library,
the 200,000 parchments

that Anthony gave
to Cleopatra

as a wedding gift.
Twilight pours over

the temples of Demeter, Hera,
and Dionysus, you imagine them

red-orange in their cold,
burning marble

as half the planet
passes into the dark.

And down the hillside
at the bridge over the river

a cathedral of red clay
disappears into shadow.

    *

This would be
    the most sacred site

of all, that
of the

consummate
    goddess

—an estimation
you share with Emperor Hadrian

who brought Isis
     out of Egypt,

built the "Red Basilica"
     (the canals inside it

     simulate
     the flooding of the Nile).

Who raised up,
     underground,

     dark chambers for such
     ritual as befits the worship of

the Queen of Heaven,
     her secrets held within

a quickly deepening red,
                walls and arches

the color of blood
            spilling onto raw

earth, here where
        the curse of incarnation

is lifted, where
Apuleius

saw the truth:
            the soul

                flies from
                    one body

        into
        another.

Asia Minor

Could be
an intuition

coming on: if one is detached,
amasses facts, passes on

what is heard with
the right mix of

credulity and
skepticism,

the shape of time
will shine forth.

    *

Could be
the historian of

what wars have made this world,
of the dynasties that now

organize all, and
control all, is

what you are
beginning to be.

＊

Could be
you will explain

strange rites in far places.
Could be you will

elucidate
rumors,

will overflow
the scroll of the known

with
wonders.

＊

You too could be
        passing through Sardis.

You too could be stepping, right now,
through the trickling

meanders of a drizzle
antiquity knew as

a surging river,
amid road dust,

and goats, curious,
still, about Croesus . . .

    *

You too could prove to be
the father of lies.

    *

(Drawn
    as you are

to the agony of
           contradiction.

    *

Dazzled
as you are by

the ambiguous grace of
                  light and dark.

               *

You often feel
less like

Herodotus
than like his friend

the dramatist,
Sophocles.

               *

               Or, more exactly,
               like a banished and

               blind king in
               one of his plays.

               As if in your knotted
               wandering you

might wind up
in a grove

where the gods
will finally

release you,
take you

into
the sky.)

Could be
these notes will be

seen someday
to have gathered all that

was understood
of the world

as it was
in our time.

＊

Or if not understood
then at least

all that once
was put

forth
as true.

*

Could be
these

desultory
jottings, these

dashed-off scraps,
will at the end of this epoch,

at the return of
eternity, be all the

information
there is, be

the sole
record of

what took place
in the world,

the world as it
once was,

be the sole
record of

your life and
what took place

within
it:

*

A few
events,

a belief or two,
a number of dreams.

Raki

Take in
this paradise

of apricots, of figs
of cucumbers,

of fertile
hills,

of streams
that once poured

alluvial gold
into the

legendary
coffers

of Croesus.
See, and taste.

Take
notes so

this might be
recalled amid

the ever-deepening
destitution of

future
days.

Sip, at night, that
miraculous

clarity
culled from

anise that when
water

is added,
turns

the glass
milky white.

homage to Herodotus

The dreams
that came to you

in Asia Minor were
admittedly nothing like

those of Astyages,
who saw a flood of

urine drench all
the city, then all Asia

and was afraid, and asked
the magi what it meant,

that it was his daughter's
and dreamed later

of a vine spilling out
from her womb and

covering all Asia,
and so ordered

that the infant
Cyrus be slain;

or of Sethos, told by
gods in a dream

they'd protect him
the night before battle

a swarm of rats ate
the bowstrings

and the scabbards
of his enemy;

or of Xerxes, driven by
a dream to attack Greece

and so his reign
brought him to ruin;

or any other of
the kind of dream

so apparently pervasive
in the classical world

where every dream leads
directly to fortune or disaster.

In fact, in all your travels,
in all your nights in

these kingdoms,
only one dream

survived waking,
blown in on a breeze

from medieval Persia.
No promise or threat

could be drawn from it.
It was a dream about

little more than
the ecstasy of art:

*

A high dome of
white marble aglow

with joyful figuration
above walls of whirls of

cobalt blue script
vines, tulips,

nymphs, satyrs
all ascending.

In sleep you're able
to look up without

pain, able to
become lost in

an architectural
reverie designed

not by a caliph from
a glorious Renaissance

Byzantium but by
a Greek surrealist,

never of course
actually built

and so your dream is
not really a dream

but a dream
of a dream of a

palazzo of pure thought,
an erotic mosque,

a cosmos con-
secrated to beauty,

a heaven
of annihilation

opening
for whoever

studies the depth of the dome,
whoever looks up

hopeless
and bereft.

Dream of
a dip

of floating
face to the sky

in the updraft of
the heat of bright sand

on the floor of the
ocean so close

below, the
body mid-

point between
earth and sky, held in

warm
shallows,

the pain pulling
away,

into the deep,
a heel grazing the sand

now and
then,

the whole
spinal cord

loosening
in

the drift, in
the healing sea,

the
Aegean.

the Temple of Apollo at Dydima

Long ago
the truest part of you

some part within a part
some most interior

most ethereal
part within a part

within a part
began to approach

the condition of stone.
So this must be, for you,

a compelling stop
on the tour,

not for the immense
and chilling pillars of

this solemn ruin
that was once, after all,

the heart
of antiquity,

but for
this Gorgon face

in a frieze,
Medusa.

Long ago
you gazed, you

were breathless,
held in place. Beauty

beset you.
By the end of that

instant you
were

ready
to worship, to be

transformed,
though it turns out

such change can take
years,

decades, in fact.
You looked

at some pained,
angry, ravishing and

sorrowful face
and asked

nothing else
but the ecstasy of

becoming
dead to

all other
love.

Sanctuary of Asclepius

Be assured, rocks
and seas will

arise from your
scattering.

    *

Till then, lie
on a slab of cloud,

on a toppled pearl-grey
beam cut with

Greek letters in
a ruined pharmacy.

    *

Here where the afflicted once
arrived, prayed, paid,

lay down, waited
for the gift of a

healing
reprieve.

*

Though it's late
in a long day,

dawn glows
between your bones;

your spine is a
horizon about to be

reborn in flame.
No sleep now.

You seem to be
awakening.

*

Pain arrives
as a radiance, as

the touch of an otherwise
hidden truth at work in the world,

a force proved now
in solitude, in

your own nerves, and again
amid crowds, by all

who limp, wince,
pause, bend, gasp, deny,

hide, accept, falter, wracked by
age, by illness, or just

twisting in
distress,

who, were they here, in the
vacancy, in the shadows of this once

holy spa, were this,
that is, still a destination

spot for
the sick and

dying, might be
heard to pray: "Heal me."

to Apollo

Before the day
dies and the night

rises up over all: heal us.
Before the hills spill down

into the draining light: heal us.
Before the world ends,

before the gods go,
before creation

fails: heal us, heal us,
heal us, the way the grief of

the sky is healed by
the ocean, the way

the torment of the sun
is healed by the dark.

JOSEPH DONAHUE was born in 1954 in Dallas and grew up in Lowell, Massachusetts. He was educated at Dartmouth College and Columbia University. He has lived in New York City and Seattle, and now makes his home in Durham, North Carolina, where he is Professor of the Practice in the English Department at Duke University.